SALADIN

KV-524-409

Written & illustrated by

Marion Khalidi

HOOD HOOD BOOKS

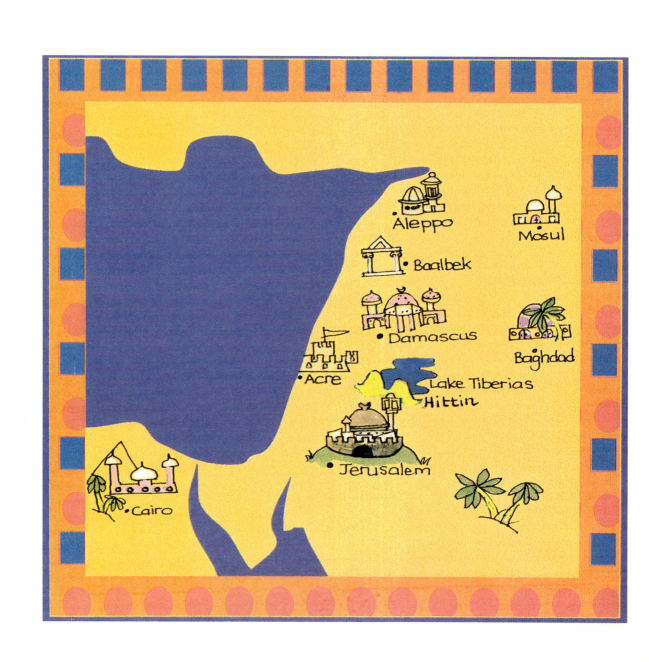

SALADIN

THE world into which Saladin was born in 1138 was a troubled and dangerous one. There were two Caliphs ruling over the Muslim world, one in Baghdad, the other in Cairo, and their followers quarrelled constantly amongst themselves. They were so busy fighting that they did not realise the more serious threat of the Crusaders.

The Crusaders, who were known as the Franks, were European Christians with a religious belief that Jerusalem and the Holy Land belonged to them. In 1099, the Crusaders had invaded and, over the years, had taken over large parts of the Eastern Mediterranean coast including Jerusalem, and had posed a threat to the whole area. Since Jerusalem was one of the most holy places in the Muslim world, it was a severe loss and the Muslims longed for its return. Saladin was destined to play a vital role in all these struggles and he became one of Islam's greatest military commanders as well as one of the most chivalrous leaders the world has ever known.

Saladin was born in the little town of Takrit, in what is now called Iraq. His father, Ayyub, was the Governor. When Saladin was a young boy, the whole family went to live in Damascus in Syria. Here, his father was put in charge of the city's citadel by Zangi who was the most powerful Muslim military leader of the time. Both Saladin's father and uncle, Shirkuh, were officers in Zangi's army.

Damascus was one of the most famous seats of learning, and an ideal place for Saladin to go to school. Even as a young boy he was fond of books, especially poetry. Although born a Kurd, Saladin's education was in Arabic and he thought of himself as a Muslim first and Kurdish second. He was able to recite passages from the Qur'an, as well as poems, and he knew all about Arab history. Saladin never imagined that he would become famous throughout the world, not as a scholar or a poet, but as a soldier and a warrior.

When Zangi died, one of his sons, Nur al-Din, took control of much of his army. Nur al-Din was an ambitious man but also a pious one. He was the first leader to alert the Muslims to the dangers of the Crusaders and to call for a holy war against the invaders.

He was aware however, that unless the Muslims stopped fighting amongst themselves, the Crusaders would never be driven out. The thing that bothered Nur al-Din most was that the whole of Egypt was under the control of the Fatimids who were constantly plotting against his own master, the Caliph of Baghdad. They had even gone as far as entering into

an alliance with the Crusaders. In 1164, Nur al-Din sent Saladin's uncle Shirkuh at the head of an army to drive the Crusaders out of Egypt. It was going to be a long and bloody campaign and Shirkuh needed courageous men on whom he could rely. He now turned to his nephew Saladin to accompany him. At first, Saladin was reluctant. Although he could ride, he was not a soldier, and preferred books to fighting. However, he could not turn down his uncle's request, and so he found himself armed and mounted, leaving Damascus and wondering whether he would ever again return to his books of poetry.

In those days, soldiers fought on foot and on horseback. They carried lances, maces and swords and wore chain mail and heavy plate armour. Archers fired arrows from behind the lines and sometimes there was single-handed combat known as the *barraz*. The ease of life in Damascus was replaced by the hardship of battles and campaigns. For four years Shirkuh, with Saladin by his side, fought battle after battle, first with the Fatimids, then with the Crusaders. It required tremendous courage to overcome the constant danger, the fierce sun, as well as the hunger and thirst. During these four years, Saladin suffered terrible hardships which he never forgot.

Eventually the Crusaders were driven out of Egypt, and Shirkuh became the Vizier which was the most important position in the country. Shirkuh may have been Saladin's uncle, but he did not possess any of his nephew's nobility. He was a short, angry man who was also very greedy and enjoyed eating huge meals. After one of his enormous meals, he had a hot bath, collapsed and died. Saladin was made Vizier in his place.

Saladin found himself in a position which he had not sought but which he had to fill. Egypt was a difficult land to rule and was as divided as the rest of the Muslim world. Although he was a good and popular Vizier, and treated the Egyptians well and fairly, he had made many enemies, some amongst his own followers. Once a ragged beggar was seen by a guard carrying a pair of brand new sandals. This looked odd and the guard took the sandals and investigated. Inside he found a concealed message inviting the Crusaders to invade.When they tracked down the scribe who had written the note, he promptly confessed and revealed the whole plot.

Saladin continued to rule wisely. He built a citadel, religious colleges, as well as an aqueduct. In 1173, his father died and then the next year, Nur al-Din also died. Nur al-Din's heir, al-Salih, was only eleven when he was left in charge, and everyone tried to take advantage of him. Saladin wrote very sternly to al-Salih's courtiers warning them to behave, but his words fell on deaf ears and he left Egypt for Syria to try and look after the young king.

And so Saladin returned to Damascus, though this time not as a young scholar and poet, but as Vizier of Egypt with 700 horsemen riding behind him. In the meantime, al-Salih, who had fallen under the control of his uncle, now raised a large army and set out to fight Saladin. Saladin therefore found himself fighting against Nur al-Din's son. His soldiers were battle-hardened and he quickly took the major cities of Syria. But Saladin was generous in victory. When Nur al-Din's young daughter came to his camp to plead for favourable terms, Saladin, who was known to be kind to

the weak and very fond of children, was so moved by the child that he showered her with presents and gave back most of the towns he had taken! The fighting with Nur al-Din's son saddened Saladin as he saw it as a distraction from his main aim of driving the Crusaders out of the Holy Land and regaining Jerusalem for Islam. Now, having united Syria and Egypt, the Crusaders were enclosed on every side by a hostile Muslim empire. For many years an uneasy truce existed between the Muslims and the Crusaders. Although Saladin wished more than anything to regain Jerusalem, he was a man of honour and he respected the terms of the truce. Reginald of Chatillon, on the other hand, Saladin's Frank neighbour, had no such sense of honour. On many occasions he had broken the terms of the truce by capturing defenceless caravans heading for Mecca, and massacring people and pillaging their goods. But on one occasion he went too far. When news reached Reginald of a Muslim caravan travelling by night, he ordered at once that it should be attacked, believing that it was laden with gold. Little did he know that the caravan was transporting something far more precious to Saladin, for travelling in it was Saladin's own sister. There could be no greater insult than attacking the honour of his family, and Saladin vowed that he would kill Reginald should he ever fall into his hands.

Reginald's insult made Saladin more determined than ever to drive the Crusaders out of the Holy Land. He gathered together an enormous army and marched against them. The two armies finally met in July 1187 in an

enclosed valley near the Horns of Hittin, a pair of hills in the area of Tiberias in Northern Palestine.

The Crusaders were camped next to a dry well and were without water. Saladin's army set fire to the brushwood, causing thick smoke to fill the air. The Crusaders were tired, thirsty and terribly hot in their heavy armour, and Saladin's army had them surrounded. He had also posted his forces in front of Lake Tiberias cutting them off from the water. There followed a terrible battle in which 10,000 Crusaders were slain and their leaders either killed or taken prisoner.

Amongst the prisoners were King Guy of Jerusalem and Reginald, who were escorted into Saladin's tent. Saladin was well known for his fair treatment of prisoners and offered the King some water but declined to give any to his hated enemy Reginald. Since he had sworn to kill him he could not offer him hospitality. Instead, he gave him the choice between converting to Islam or death. Reginald chose death and was slain.

Upon witnessing this, King Guy thought that he too would be slain, but Saladin reassured him: *It is not the custom of kings to slay kings but this man has gone beyond all bounds.*

The Battle of Hittin was a great victory for Saladin and a crushing blow for the Crusaders. The road to Jerusalem lay open. At the head of his army, Saladin now entered it victorious, claiming it back for the Muslims on October 2nd, 1187. Once again, Saladin was generous in victory, and he let all the Crusaders go free. The soldiers in Jerusalem were allowed to leave with their women and children and although there was a ransom fixed on their heads, Saladin himself is said to have paid the ransom for thousands of people to go free.

At the moment of his greatest triumph, alarming news reached Saladin. It appeared that King Guy, whose life Saladin had spared on the condition that he return to Europe, had gone back on his word and had instead seized the port of Acre.

He had been joined there by Richard, the King of England, known as

Richard the Lionheart. At once, Saladin set off, but the scene which greeted him was so shocking that he could not help but weep. The city had been sacked and its Muslim population massacred. So furious were the Franks at losing Jerusalem that not even the animals were spared.

During the next few months the Muslim and Christian armies were locked in battle. At the head of the Crusader army stood Richard the Lionheart, who, although not as chivalrous or honourable as Saladin, matched him for courage and bravery. Richard was determined to re-capture Jerusalem and Saladin was equally determined to prevent him from doing so.

Saladin and Richard never actually met each other, but Saladin knew what was taking place in the camp of the English king. One day, news reached him that Richard had fallen seriously ill with a fever. In those days, Muslim doctors were advanced in medicine; Saladin himself had an excellent personal doctor called Sheikh Jarrah whom he sent to treat Richard. The doctor did not go empty-handed, and took with him a small gift, a bowl of fruit sherbet kept cold in an ice bucket filled with snow from the mountains of Lebanon. Richard was very touched and accepted gratefully both the gift and the medicine - which helped to cure him.

15

Eventually, Richard tired of war and tried to make peace with Saladin. There was even a plan to marry Saladin's brother to Richard's sister so that they would rule jointly over Jerusalem allowing both Crusaders and Muslims free access to the city. But Richard's sister did not like the idea and nothing came of it. Eventually, after many negotiations, a peace treaty was signed. This treaty allowed each side to go into the territory of the other without fear, and at last Richard returned home.

After Richard's departure, Saladin rested for a while in Jerusalem where he built a hospital and a religious college. Now that the Crusaders had been driven out, and Jerusalem had been regained, he decided to return to Damascus, the city of his youth, where he had been happiest. Finally, he could return to his books and poetry! It was in Damascus that Saladin died in 1193.

Saladin was not only a great general, but also a learned and humane man. He built many mosques and citadels that stll stand today in cities such as Cairo and Aleppo. He built hospitals and schools and encouraged religious knowledge and belief. His friends said he was tender-hearted despite being a brave warrior. Even amongst the Crusaders, he was known for his chivalry and for always keeping his word. Women and children were treated well and any who were taken prisoner were reunited with their families.

Before his death, Saladin gave away large amounts of money to charity and the poor so that when he finally died, he left only a tiny sum of money. His suit of mail and his charger were all the property he had left.

Today, Saladin's name lives on as an example of bravery and chivalry throughout the world.

HEROES FROM THE EAST

· SALADIN ·

MARION KHALIDI

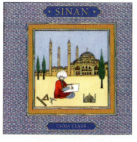

· SINAN ·

EMMA CLARK

QUEEN OF SHEBA

MARION KHALIDI

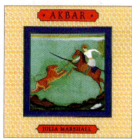

· AKBAR ·

JULIA MARSHALL

· CHENG HO ·

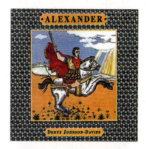

· ALEXANDER ·

DENYS JOHNSON-DAVIES

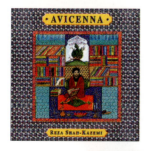

· AVICENNA ·

REZA SHAH-KAZEMI

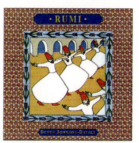

· RUMI ·

DENYS JOHNSON-DAVIES

· CLEOPATRA ·
QUEEN OF KINGS

Abd al-Rahman Azzam

· MEHMET ·
THE CONQUEROR

Emma Clark

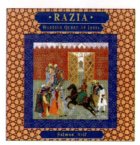

· RAZIA ·
WARRIOR QUEEN OF INDIA

Salma Asif